Florence Rena Sabin:
Pioneer Scientist

Acknowledgments

We want to thank the following people for sharing with us their professional expertise and for their kindness and encouragement in this project.

Catherine Engel, Librarian, Documentary Resources, Colorado Historical Society.

Jane Fitz-Randolph, Author and Teacher.

Nancy Markham, Curator of Education, Colorado Historical Society.

Roger Martinez, Director, Multi-Ethnic Studies, Colorado Department of Education.

Judy Volc, Children's Librarian, Boulder Public Library.

Florence Rena Sabin: Pioneer Scientist

WRITTEN BY **SYBIL DOWNING**
AND **JANE VALENTINE BARKER**

Illustrations by Ann Jones

PRUETT **PUBLISHING COMPANY**
Boulder, Colorado

©1981 By Sybil Downing and Jane Valentine Barker
All rights reserved, including those to reproduce
this book, or parts thereof, in any form, without
permission in writing from the Publisher.

First Edition

1 2 3 4 5 6 7 8 9

Printed in the United States of America

Library of Congress Cataloging in Publication Data

Downing, Sybil.
  Florence Rena Sabin, pioneer scientist.

  Bibliography: p.
  1. Sabin, Florence Rena, 1871-1953.
2. Anatomists—United States—Biography.
I. Title.
QM16.S23D68   611'.0092'4   [B]   81-8486
ISBN 0-87108-237-3 (pbk.)   AACR2

Contents

The Move to Denver 1
Growing Up for Florence 9
A New Family 19
Discovering the Past 27
Back with Mary 35
What to do Next 43
Big Decisions 49
New Adventures 57
The Real Test 63
Florence Finds Her Niche 71
A Friend is Lost 77
Honors and Changes 81
Another Adventure 89
A Wonderful End 93

The Move to Denver

Fall 1875

Florence Sabin peeked through the picket fence around their yard. Living in Denver was different from living in Central City, she thought. No mountains to climb or wild flowers to pick for Mama.

But there were Indians. Today she and her older sister, Mary, would watch them as they rode by on their ponies from their camp on the edge of town to the business part of Denver. Papa said the Indians were mostly Utes and Arapahoes. Florence liked to wave at the boys and girls. Maybe one of them would wave back today.

"Mama, can we go watch the Indians now?" called Florence as she dashed through the front door of the small brick house.

Mama was combing Mary's hair into long smooth curls. "Not this morning, dear," she replied. "You have to change your dress. Don't you remember, we're going to take Mary to see her new school?"

"My school, too," reminded Florence.

"Now, Florence," said Mama. "I have already explained that you can't go to school until you're six. But you're right—some day it will be your school, too. So I think you will like seeing it, don't you?"

Florence just nodded as her mother started to unbutton her dress for her.

"Here, Florence, turn around," said Mama as she helped Florence into her clean clothes. "I want to retie that bow on your pinafore." Both girls loved the starchy white pinafores their mother made for them to wear over their gingham dresses.

"There now," said Mama, giving the bow a pat. "I guess we're ready. Mary, you hold Florence's hand. It's worth your life to cross the street, what with all these carriages and wagons here in Denver."

The Sabin family had just moved to Denver from Central City. Papa managed mines throughout the Rocky Mountains and said it would be easier to live in Denver now.

George Sabin had come to Central City from Vermont during the first gold strike over ten years ago. After awhile the gold lying in the streams played out, and most of the miners left. But George Sabin decided to stay. He wanted to try to mine the gold he felt sure was lying deep within the mountain rocks. Other men stayed for the same reason. Soon the little town of Central City grew.

A young school teacher, also from Vermont, moved to the neighboring town of Blackhawk. Serena Miner was her name. Her dark brown hair hung in curls to her shoulders. Not long after they met, George Sabin and Serena Miner found they both loved the mountains and each other. They were married in 1867. Their first child, Mary, was born two years later. And Florence was born in 1871.

Now Florence was four years old. She and Mary went everywhere together. Hand in hand the two girls skipped down the street ahead of their mother. Soon Florence could see a two-story brick building. Children were playing in the yard outside. That must be the Broadway School, thought Florence. Her school.

As they started up the curved walk, Florence stopped skipping and walked in the shadow of her mother's skirts. But Mary grabbed Florence's hand again and pulled her toward a group of children.

"Good morning," said her mother to a woman standing on the steps. "I am Mrs. Sabin, and I have brought our daughter, Mary, who is starting first grade."

"And me, too," reminded Florence. The woman on the stairs smiled down at her.

"How do you do. I'm Miss Thurman, one of the teachers," she explained, patting Florence's curly hair.

Florence didn't really like grownups patting her. As she ducked, she noticed that most of the boys and girls were lined up by a bucket set on a wooden bench.

A boy stepped up to the bucket and, taking the dipper from the girl ahead of him, he pushed it into the water in the bucket. Gulping down the water, he wiped off his wet mouth with the back of his hand and handed the dipper to the boys waiting behind him.

"Mama, I'm thirsty," said Florence. "May I get some water from the bucket over there?"

"I should say not," stated Mama. "You can have some when we get home." She turned to the teacher.

"Miss Thurman," said Mama quietly. "I can't believe you allow all the children to drink from the same dipper and the same bucket of water."

"Why, Mrs. Sabin," the tall woman answered. "What can possibly be the harm of it? I never let any of the children stand over the bucket when they drink. So none of the water drips into the bucket."

Raising her eyebrows, Mama said nothing. But she stared at the line of boys and girls by the bucket.

"Anyway," continued Miss Thurman. "We'll look forward to having Mary with us on Monday." She turned to Florence. "Perhaps you also will be one of our first graders in a year or two."

Florence looked up at her mother. Why couldn't she go to school with Mary this year? Not wait a year or two.

"Perhaps so," answered Mama. Taking Florence's hand, she led the girls back down the sidewalk toward home.

"Mama—" began Florence.

"I know, dear," Mama replied. "You counted on going to school with Mary. But four years old is just too young. You and I will have lots of things to do together while Mary is at school. You'll see."

Florence hung her head and stabbed the toes of her shoes in the dust of the street. Four wasn't too young, she thought. She already knew her alphabet.

"Besides, girls," said Mama. "I'm not so sure about that school."

Florence looked up. "Why, Mama?" she asked.

"Well, letting those children drink from that one bucket with that one dipper just won't do."

"Oh," said Florence. She wondered why it wouldn't do. The water looked fine to her.

Wiping their feet on the mat outside the front door, Mary and Florence followed their mother into their little house.

"Come into the kitchen, girls," said Mama. "I want to show you something."

Reaching up into the cupboard, Mama took down two glasses. She went to the sink and began to work the handle of the water pump up and down. Soon the water splashed out. Filling each glass, she handed one to Mary and one to Florence.

"There, you see," said Mama. "Each of you

has your own glass with fresh, clean water. And no one else will drink from your glass. All your lives I want you girls to remember not to drink out of any one else's cup, no matter how clean it looks."

"Yes, Mama," answered Mary.

Florence nodded. Mama always cared about things being clean. Florence knew that. But now Mama said not to drink from someone else's glass even when the water looked perfectly clean. That seemed strange. She wasn't sure she really understood. But if Mama said it, it must be right.

Florence guessed that Mama was probably also right that just the two of them would have fun together—even without Mary.

Growing Up for Florence

Spring 1876

Mama was right. Early one spring morning Florence and Mary stood in Mama and Papa's bedroom.

"Would you like to hold your new baby brother now, Florence?" asked Papa.

Florence was so excited she could only nod. Papa placed a bundle of lacey blanket in her arms. Carefully he pulled the blanket open. Looking down, Florence could see him now. Little Richman.

"Mama," she whispered. "He's so tiny. Do you think he knows I'm his big sister?"

Mama was lying against several pillows in the big bed. The baby had been born very early that morning. Now everyone wanted to see the new member of the family.

"No, dear," she replied. "I don't think Richman knows much of anything yet. You will have to help me teach him, you know."

"Mama is right, Florence," said Papa, putting his arm around her. "Now that I must travel so much from one mine to the next and

Mary is in school, you must be Mama's helper."

Papa took Richman from Florence and gently placed him in the cradle next to Mama's bed. "Now, girls," he said, "I think Mama needs to rest. You can help by heating her some of the soup the neighbors left us."

Florence and Mary tiptoed out of the room and quietly closed the door. Mary placed some small sticks of wood in the fire box to start the stove, just as she had seen Mama do so often. Because Mama had to rest now, Florence thought she and Mary would be doing a lot of the cooking.

A pottery bowl covered with a white towel sat on the kitchen table. Mary reached into the cupboard and found a pot. She carefully ladled some of the soup into it.

"The soup should be ready pretty soon, Florence," said Mary. "Maybe Mama would like a piece of that nut bread someone brought." She unwrapped the loaf and sliced off a piece.

Dripping a little water onto her finger tips, Mary tossed the drops across the stove top. The beads of water sizzled as they danced over the black surface.

"You can put the soup on the stove, Florence. It's ready now," said Mary in a grownup way. Sometimes Mary was just a little bossy, Florence thought.

Florence held the handle of the pot with

both hands and carefully lifted it to the stove. She pulled a wooden chair up to the stove. When she stood on the seat of the chair, she was tall enough to stir the soup so it didn't burn on the bottom.

"Mama wouldn't like you to stand on a chair," reminded Mary, sternly.

"Maybe not," answered Florence. "But it's not my fault if I'm so short. Anyway, I'm helping."

From then on, Florence helped Mama often. Sometimes Mama let her help give Richman a bath. Florence loved to see his tiny hands and feet splashing in the warm sudsy water as their mother held him in the wash tub.

If the days were warm, Florence pushed Richman in his baby carriage around the neighborhood. The lady living at the corner always came out to see Richman. "What a beautiful baby," she would say. Florence would smile and answer, "He's my baby brother, you know."

Florence was so busy sweeping the floors and taking care of Richman that she almost didn't notice Christmas was coming. One cold, windy day, Papa burst through the front door, his arms full of packages.

"Do you know what tomorrow is, girls?" he asked.

"Why, it's Christmas, Papa," answered Mary, laughing.

"And so it is," he said. He picked Florence up, tossing her above his head. "My, what a big girl you are getting to be! Won't be too much longer before you're a school girl like Mary, will it?"

"Well, if I have time, Papa," Florence answered solemnly. "I'm very busy with Richman."

"Oh, I know you are, dear," he answered. "Mama says she couldn't do without you."

"But we have no time for talking," said Papa. "Right now we have to put up our tree. I brought one all the way from Central City."

"Oh, Papa," said Mary, "This is going to be the best Christmas ever."

As Papa put up the tree, Mama brought out bowls of dried fruit and popcorn to string as decoration for the tree.

"This calls for a song," said Papa. He laughed his cheery laugh. "What shall we sing?"

"*Jingle Bells*?" suggested Florence.

"*Jingle Bells* it is," answered Papa.

Florence loved to hear Papa sing. His voice was deep and warm. As they all sang, Papa went over to Mama once in awhile to put his arm around her waist. Even baby Richman gurgled happily as he lay in his basket.

Christmas was a wonderful day. Florence found a beautiful pair of mittens in her package.

She and Mary had pressed some flowers for Mama.

The days were too cold now for Florence to take Richman out very often. Instead she played with him indoors while Mama made bread or did the washing.

One day Richman started to cough. His little face would turn red and then purple. Florence picked him up and patted him on his back. After awhile he stopped coughing. But the next day he was coughing even more. That night as Florence lay next to Mary in their bed, she could hear Mama walking around the house, and she could hear Richman coughing.

The next morning she got up early. She remembered how Mama sometimes gave her or Mary honey when they had a cough. Maybe Richman would like some honey.

She pulled on her wool stockings and pushed her feet into her high-top shoes. She couldn't button her dress up in the back, but that was all right. Mama would do that later.

As she tiptoed toward the kitchen, she noticed the kerosene lamp burning. Then she saw Mama hunched over as she sat in one of the kitchen chairs. Papa had his arms around her.

Florence blinked as she came into the lighted kitchen. "Papa, what's wrong?" she asked. "Is Richman sicker?"

"Richman is all right now, Florence," said

her father quietly. "You see, God took him from us last night to live with Him in heaven."

"What do you mean, Papa?" asked Florence.

"Papa means, Florence dear," Mama said as she straightened up for a minute, "that Richman died early this morning."

Just then Mary came through the doorway. "But why, Mama?" she asked.

"He was very sick, dear," said Mama, wiping her reddened eyes with her handkerchief. "There was nothing we could do to help him."

Florence looked first at Mama and then at Papa. She felt a big lump in her throat. She squeezed her eyes shut very tight for a minute. Then she turned and ran from the room.

Throwing herself on the bed, she began to sob. She could feel Mary sit down beside her.

"It's not fair, Mary," she cried. "It's just not fair. Richman was our baby. We want him. Why should God have him?"

Mary didn't say anything. She blew her nose.

Papa came in and sat down on the edge of the bed. He gathered the two girls into his arms.

"Now, girls," he said. "This is a very, very sad day. We all loved Richman very much. But we will go on."

"Will we ever have another little brother, Papa," asked Florence, wiping her eyes with the back of her hand.

"Well, it's hard to say, dear," he said, gently. "But perhaps some day."

That some day came sooner than Florence and Mary thought possible. Just two weeks before Florence's seventh birthday, baby Albert was born.

Florence knew how to care for babies now, so Mama let her and Mary take care of Albert most of the time. Mama did not get out of bed very often. Her skin looked white as chalk, and Florence noticed her pretty dark eyes didn't sparkle much any more.

The girls tiptoed around the house as they swept and cleaned. Florence could make stew now. And Mary learned to bake the bread.

The night before her birthday as Florence lay in bed, she wondered if Papa brought her anything from his last trip to Leadville. Being seven years old was rather important, she thought; she had started school last month; and she even skipped to second grade because she could read so well. Soon her eyes grew heavy and she fell asleep.

The next thing she knew, Papa was leaning over the bed. "Girls, wake up," he said. "I have to talk to you about something."

Both girls turned sleepily toward their father. Florence sat up in bed, rubbing her eyes.

"What is it, Papa?" she asked.

"Well, you remember how Richman went to

live with God in heaven?" he asked.

Mary nodded.

"Last night Mama left us, too," he said quietly, looking down at his hands.

"Mama? Dead?" gasped Mary.

Papa only nodded.

"First Richman. Now Mama," Florence whispered. She could feel the tears slipping down her cheeks. "God isn't fair. What will we do without her?"

"We will just have to manage somehow," explained Papa. "Uncle Albert and some of your aunts will be here in a few days. We will decide where you girls will live then. And I will get a nurse to care for baby Albert, I suppose. I just have no way to take care of you all now."

Florence slid out of bed and ran from the room and down the hall to the kitchen. She could hardly breathe. As she pumped the handle of the water spigot, she thought of Mama. She filled her own glass with clear, cold water. She would always remember Mama.

Looking out the window, she saw the bright yellow leaves dancing in the fall breeze as they hung from the branches of the small trees in the back yard.

Then she remembered. Today was her birthday. Her seventh birthday. October 31. The last day she would ever be a little girl again, she thought.

A New Family

November 1879

Papa had decided that Mary and Florence should go to Wolfe Hall, a girls' school in Denver. Wolfe Hall was a boarding school where the students lived and went to school, too.

Bishop Spaulding was the principal of the school. He was a nice man, thought Florence. She liked the two Spaulding girls and their brother. They had all been kind when she and Mary came to live at Wolfe Hall over a year ago. But it just wasn't the same without Papa and baby Albert.

Tonight Florence turned over in bed quietly. Mary slept beside her. Florence was thinking about Mama and Richman. She pushed her face into the pillow so no one would hear her cry.

Florence could hear the cook heating the stove downstairs. Soon Mrs. Spaulding bustled up the stairs to wake the students whose rooms were on the second floor.

Now the slightly round little lady was standing over the girls' bed. "Florence, Mary," she said, shaking them by the shoulders. "Do come downstairs right away. Bishop Spaulding wishes to speak to both of you about something."

Almost at once both girls sat up and looked at each other. Florence just knew something was wrong again. Silently, they both dressed and went downstairs to the library.

Bishop Spaulding was a large man with a balding head. He always puffed a pipe. Now he sat, looking out the window, in a large chair behind his desk. When he heard Florence and Mary come into the booklined room, he turned around.

"Come in, my dears," he said kindly. "Do sit down. I'm afraid I have some bad news and some good news for you."

Florence and Mary didn't say a word, but just looked at each other.

"I am saddened to tell you that your little brother, Albert, passed away yesterday. Pneumonia, the doctors said it was," he added.

Florence clenched her fists. She could hear Mary suck in her breath.

"The good news is that your Uncle Albert will be coming to take you to live with him and his lovely family in Chicago," explained Bishop Spaulding.

"And Papa?" asked Florence. "Why can't we live with Papa again?"

"Well, your father sent word that he loves you both very much," said the large man. "But he feels living in the mountains would be too hard for you young ladies. You will be much happier with your Uncle Albert."

Florence hung her head and tried to remember Uncle Albert. He had come to Mama's funeral. He looked a lot like Papa. Mama had once told them he was a teacher in Chicago. Florence thought he had a son about Mary's age.

"We thank you very much for telling us, Bishop Spaulding," Florence heard Mary saying.

"Now you girls must be brave," he replied. "Perhaps after school today, you would be wise

to start packing your things."

A week later, after a long train ride across the prairies, Florence and Mary climbed down the steep steps of the railroad car onto the platform of the Chicago railroad station. Florence thought it looked like a big cave.

A tall man pushed his way through the crowd. "Florence! Mary!" he called out. "I'm your Uncle Albert. Remember?"

Florence was right. He did look like Papa.

In a short time the three of them stepped out of a carriage and stood before a sturdy wooden house. A little woman with her blond hair bound in a soft knot at the nape of her neck came out the front door. She held open her arms.

"Oh, my dears," she said warmly. "Here you are at last! Come in and have some hot chocolate."

She started to help Florence unbutton her coat and unwrap Mary's long muffler. "Isn't this November weather in Chicago terrible?" she said. "Come and warm yourselves by the stove."

Before Florence knew it, she was sitting at a kitchen table, her cold hands wrapped around a warm mug of hot chocolate. Just like home, with Mama. But she decided not to think about that.

In a few minutes Uncle Albert came into the kitchen. A tall boy with brown curly hair followed him.

"Mary and Florence," he said in his booming voice. "This is your cousin Stewart. I know you three will be good friends."

Stewart smiled. "I'm glad you're here, Florence and Mary," he said. "Do you play the piano?"

The girls looked at each other. "I'm afraid not," said Mary.

"Well, you sing, don't you?" he asked. "All Sabins sing."

Florence and Mary nodded. They hadn't sung together for a very long time.

"Now Margaret," said Uncle Albert, "if you will pour Stewart and me a mug of warm chocolate and join us with a mug yourself, I think we will be ready for a song—to celebrate this fine day."

Florence began to tingle. Maybe it was the warmth of the stove. Maybe it was Uncle Albert's warm voice.

"I will choose the song," he said. " 'We Gather Together to Ask the Lord's Blessing,' is a fine song for this important day, I think."

Stewart took a small silver pitch pipe from his pocket. "Stewart, give us the pitch, if you please," Uncle Albert said.

Stewart blew through the small silver pipe. Then suddenly Uncle Albert began leading them all in song. In a few minutes, just as they began the third verse, Florence felt Mary's warm hand in hers. They looked at each other and smiled. Yes, living with Uncle Albert, Aunt Margaret, and cousin Stewart would be almost like being at home.

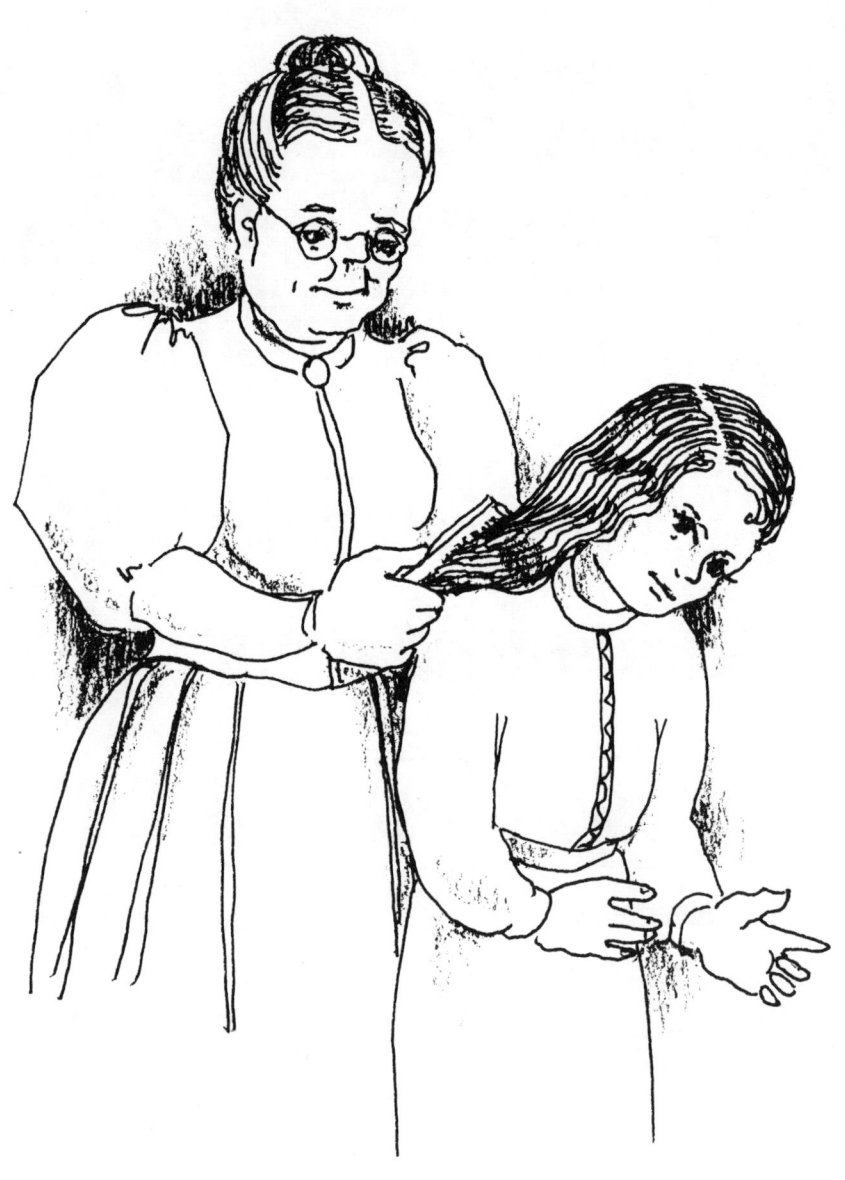

Discovering the Past

Summer 1883

Four years came and went. They were good years for Mary and Florence: years full of love, sharing good books, and learning to play the piano.

On a hot summer day in July, as they sat eating a dinner of cold chicken, Uncle Albert asked "What would all of you children think of visiting Grandfather and Grandmother Sabin in Vermont this summer?"

Mary and Florence looked at each other and then at their cousin Stewart. Vermont? What did she know about Vermont, wondered Florence? She thought maybe the Pilgrims settled there. All she really knew was that Vermont was where both her mother and father were born.

Pictures of Grandmother and Grandfather Sabin glared from the walls of the upstairs hall. Florence passed those pictures several times every day. She never thought either of them looked very friendly or even very happy. She wasn't at all sure she wanted to visit them. But she would go if Uncle Albert thought it was a good idea.

By August 1 the entire family was climbing off the train at the Rockingham, Vermont, station. As Florence looked around her, she spied an old man striding toward them. He looked almost like Papa or Uncle Albert, but he had gray hair.

"Albert, my son! Good to see you," said the man when he reached Uncle Albert. The two men shook hands.

"Father, these are George's daughters—Mary and Florence," said Uncle Albert. "And you remember Stewart."

Grandfather Sabin patted both girls on the head and put his arm around Stewart's shoulders. Then he kissed Aunt Margaret on both cheeks. "Grandmother is waiting to see all of you," he said softly. "Let's go home."

They all placed their bags in the back of the carriage, and climbed inside. With a flick of the reins, Grandfather Sabin guided the horses down the street and out of town.

Strangely, the countryside made Florence think of Colorado—maybe because it was hilly. In fact, she could even see what looked like a real mountain up ahead.

She tapped Uncle Albert's shoulder. "Is that a mountain up there?" she asked.

"It is indeed," he answered, smiling.

"Mount Ascutney. Nothing like some of the mountains you and Mary remember in Colorado, but for Vermont it's a real skyscraper."

A skyscraper. Florence thought about that as the carriage jogged along. Uncle Albert always knew just how to describe things. Mountains—high mountains, anyway—really did seem to scrape the sky. Some day she wanted to climb to the top of some of those skyscrapers.

Suddenly grandfather turned the carriage into a yard and stopped it in front of a large wooden house. "There's Grandmother waiting for us," announced Grandfather Sabin.

A small woman whose dark hair was streaked with gray was standing by the back door. "Welcome, everyone," she called. "Our home is your home."

The next morning after breakfast Florence started to run out the front door. "Just one minute, young lady," Grandmother called out firmly.

Before she let the door close behind her, Florence stopped. "Where do you think you are going?" asked Grandmother.

"I just thought I would find Uncle Albert and go flower hunting, Grandmother," she answered.

"My dear, chores first, pleasure later," said Grandmother. "There are dishes to be washed and beds to be made."

Florence sighed, turned, and came back into the house. No one argued with Grandmother.

Soon the chores were finished and the girls ran across the fields to find Uncle Albert. The song of the bobolinks filled the air in the meadows.

The entire summer seemed as if it were a magic time to Florence. Grandfather Sabin never said much, but Florence loved to watch his twinkling eyes when he told a story. Grandmother Sabin was the best cook in the world.

Every morning as she helped Mary and Florence comb their hair, Grandmother shook her head. "Just because you girls have beautiful curly hair is no reason to get swelled heads."

Florence and Mary would always look at each other and smile.

As the summer days began to grow shorter, Florence knew it was almost time for them to go back to Chicago. One night as they sat at the dining room table, Grandfather said "I would like you girls to spend the winter with your Grandmother and me."

"Would you like that?" asked Uncle Albert.

Florence glanced at Mary. "You mean we would go to school here, Grandfather?" she asked.

He smiled at her. "Yes, you would go to school here. A new girls' school has opened not too far from here. Vermont Academy, they call it. Your Uncle Albert has looked into it and thinks it's quite fine."

"But if it's just for girls, where would Stewart go to school?" asked Florence.

"Stewart would be going home with us," answered Uncle Albert.

"Oh," said Florence, quietly. She would miss Stewart.

"Well, you don't need to make up your minds now," said Grandmother. "We'll talk more in the morning."

After Florence finished wiping the last breakfast dish dry, she ran out the back door and to the rose garden. Uncle Albert was trimming off the wilted blooms.

"Do you really want us to stay with Grandfather and Grandmother?" she asked him.

He nodded. "Yes, Florence," he answered. "I think it would be a chance for you and Mary to go to a fine school, and there is a great deal your grandparents can teach you both."

Vermont Academy was in the nearby town of Saxton Rivers. The new school only had three buildings. The other girls seemed nice enough, but Florence really didn't spend much time at school with them. She and Mary came home to Grandfather and Grandmother every night.

Sometimes in the long, dark winter evenings after the supper dishes were washed and put away and after their arithmetic problems were done, Florence would listen to Grandmother tell about Papa.

"Your father was studying to be a doctor, you know," she said. "Unfortunately, though, the gold fever hit him and he went west to Central City."

Florence curled up closer to the fire. Just think, Papa might have been a doctor.

"Of course, you know that your other uncle, Uncle Robert, is a doctor," Grandmother Sabin went on to explain. "In fact, your Great Great Grandfather Levi was the first doctor in the family—way back in 1798." She nodded as she spoke. "Yes, you girls come from a fine old family."

How exciting it was, thought Florence, to know that all those people in their family had been doctors. Florence watched the yellow flames dance in the fireplace. What was ahead for her, she wondered?

Back with Mary

September 1890

Florence stared out the train window, watching the fence posts that seemed to fly by. Every so often the cinders from the engine's smokestack blew across the sunny countryside.

She was eighteen now, and sometimes her life seemed like the countryside. The black cinders were the sad things that happened—like when members of the family had died. But now she was going to college with Mary, and her life was like the sun warming those cornfields out there.

Florence thought about how Mary had graduated from Vermont Academy two years ago and gone to college. Then their grandparents had died. After that Florence lived at the school and spent the summers in Chicago with Uncle Albert.

Suddenly a voice boomed out, bringing Florence's thoughts back to the train ride. "Northhampton! Northhampton!" called out the conductor.

A girl leaned over the back of the seat. "This is our stop, Miss Sabin," she said.

"Oh, thanks," Florence replied. The other young women on the train were also going to Smith College. Maybe some of them would be in her classes.

The conductor made his way down the aisle and stopped next to Florence. He reached up to the rack above her seat. "This your carpetbag?" he asked. "I'll just get it down for you."

"Thank you very much," answered Florence, as she straightened her hat and pulled on her gloves. The young women in the car began to crowd into the aisle.

Now the train was chugging to a stop. The brakes squealed. The conductor propped open the train door and swung down from the steep steps to the station platform.

"All right, young lady, out you come," he said.

Florence grasped his hand. She took a small jump and almost landed on Mary.

"Here at last!" exclaimed her sister, giving Florence a hug. "Come on! I'll help you with your bag. We have to catch the tram to the college."

Between them, the girls dragged the bag over to a tram, filled with laughing classmates.

Florence and Mary found seats, and a moment later the tram started down the treelined street.

"Oh, isn't it wonderful to be together again?" Mary exclaimed. She squeezed Florence's hand. "It will be like old times, won't it?"

Florence smiled. The other students around them chattered happily with each other. They all seemed nice, she thought. But how did they keep their white blouses so clean after that long train ride? She tried to smooth the wrinkles out of her skirt, and she wished she had brushed the tangles out of her hair.

Soon the tram began to make stops, letting off small groups of young women and their baggage.

"Look over there," said Mary. "Tenney House! We're almost home."

Another new home, thought Florence. But what did it matter? She was with Mary now.

The girls climbed down from the tram and began to lug the carpetbag up the path toward a large white house. "Aren't we the slowpokes?" puffed Mary. "But we've almost made it. Come on and I'll show you our room. Then you can meet everyone."

Florence and Mary dragged the heavy bag up the broad wooden steps and into a big front hall. Other girls were bounding up and down the stairs.

The two girls climbed the stairs and walked down a narrow hall.

"Here we are," Mary announced, turning into a small room. Two beds, two desks, and two chairs filled the space almost to overflowing. Florence could see the limbs of a huge tree just outside the big window.

Something seemed homey about the room. Maybe she had been here before. And then she saw it.

"Oh, Mary! My bedspread! The one Grandmother made me!" exclaimed Florence. "How did you ever get it here?"

'That's a deep secret," answered Mary, smiling. "I just thought you would like it. And see the pillowcase I made? It's your favorite color—yellow, just like the bedspread."

"Now it really is home," Florence said, happily.

"Well, that settles it," replied Mary. "Time to go meet people."

Florence sat down on the bed and shook her head. "Oh, you know me and meeting new people, Mary."

"Well, you're in college now, silly," said Mary. "You have to meet new people. Anyway, a very special lady, Dr. Preston, made me promise to bring you to see her."

"Did you say a lady named Dr. Preston?"

"Yes—" replied Mary.

"But ladies aren't doctors," said Florence.

"Well, this lady is a doctor. In fact, she is the doctor for the entire college," Mary answered. "And she lives right here in Tenney House."

Florence pulled her fingers through her short curly hair. "But why would a lady doctor want to meet me?" she asked.

"Because I told her you were interested in science and things like that," explained Mary. "Now let's go."

After they were downstairs, Mary led Florence toward a large door that was partly open.

Mary knocked.

"Come in, come in, whoever you are," called a cheery voice.

Mary led Florence in to a large room lined with bookshelves. Even Uncle Albert didn't have this many books, thought Florence. A tall woman sat at a large desk covered with more books and stacks of papers.

"Mary! How nice to see you," she said, looking up. "Please excuse the mess. Always too much to read and do, and not enough time to tidy up."

"Dr. Preston, this is Florence," Mary announced.

Pushing up the glasses that were resting almost on the end of her nose, the woman looked at Florence carefully.

"Yes, I see it," she said. "Couldn't miss it for the world. A Sabin sister. A great likeness to you, Mary."

"How do you do," said Florence, almost whispering. She walked up to the desk and held out her hand.

"Oh, my dear, I am very well indeed," said Dr. Preston, laughing. She gave Florence's hand a brisk shake. "We are all so glad you will be studying here at Smith College," she continued. "And I am particularly pleased you're here. Mary says you're quite a good science student."

"I do think science is interesting," Florence replied. "Especially zoology."

"Well, after you get settled in your classes, I want you to visit me often," said Dr. Preston. "Perhaps we can talk about women who are interested in zoology."

Florence thought a lot about what Dr. Preston had said that day. However, she was so busy studying and learning how to play tennis that little time was left for visiting.

She and Mary didn't really know much about tennis, but they both were quite sure the exercise was good for them. Mary said all the girls were learning to play. So they each bought a racquet, and every afternoon they went out to hit the ball back and forth.

"This is silly!" said Florence one day. She knocked her racquet against her skirt. A cloud of dust puffed out. Dirt from the nearby fields had blown onto the clay courts. "Why in the world are we playing in the dust with these awful skirts?"

"Well, what else should we wear?" demanded Mary, her hands on her hips.

"Bloomers," answered Florence.

"Bloomers!" Mary said. "Young ladies don't wear bloomers."

"Why not?" asked Florence. "I'll bet Amelia Bloomer invented them just for things like playing tennis. And anyway, all this dust on these skirts just isn't healthy."

Mary started to laugh. "Oh, Florence! You never change," she said. "You're more interested in health than in your looks. How will you ever get a husband?"

"Who cares about a husband?" Florence said. "Anyway, I have to go study."

"No more tennis?" asked Mary.

"Not unless you find us some bloomers first," answered Florence, and she marched off toward Tenney House.

What to do Next

Spring 1893

Florence and Mary didn't get bloomers, so they didn't play much tennis. But they did take long walks through the woods nearby. They looked for new plants and flowers nestled under the bushes.

During those first two years at college, Florence did almost everything with Mary. But then Mary graduated and moved back to Denver to teach mathematics at East Denver High School.

Now Florence was all by herself. She never had much to talk about with the other girls. They were interested in boys and dances. Florence just wanted to spend time in the zoology laboratory.

One beautiful warm spring day, she was studying at her desk when she heard giggles. Looking out the window, Florence saw a group of girls lying on the grass. They were laughing and tossing bits of grass at each other. How pretty they looked, thought Florence.

She put down her pen and walked over to the mirror. She looked carefully at herself in the small mirror. Round face, small blue eyes peering through steel rimmed glasses, and curly hair that never would stay in place. I'm really not very pretty, Florence decided. Mary was right — how would she ever find a husband?

She tucked her blouse into her skirt and brushed her hair. Pulling open the door, she went downstairs.

"Dr. Preston, it's Florence. May I come in?" she called as she tapped on the door.

"I wondered when you would stop by again," said Dr. Preston, opening the door. "Do come in. You're just in time for some tea and cookies."

Florence finished the last drop of steaming tea and placed the fragile cup and saucer on the tea tray.

"It's the future I'm wondering about, Dr. Preston," she began.

"I thought it might be," replied Dr. Preston. She leaned back in the large chair.

"I mean, if a woman is not going to get married, what can she do?" asked Florence.

Dr. Preston smiled. "I know a better question: What do you—Florence Sabin—want to do?"

"Well—" Florence hesitated.

"Your zoology professor tells me you're his best student," said Dr. Preston.

Florence looked down at the floor.

"Didn't you once tell me you come from a long line of doctors?" asked Dr. Preston. "And a long line of pioneers?"

"Yes, but they were all men," replied Florence.

"Even the pioneers?" asked Dr. Preston. "What about your mother? She went west all by herself to teach school."

"That's true," admitted Florence. "But the doctors were all men." She felt her face turning red. "I know you're a doctor. But you're so unusual. I never knew a lady doctor before."

"No need to be embarrassed, Florence," replied Dr. Preston. "You're quite right. There are very few women who are doctors. Most of them had to go to school in Europe because our country does not let women into the medical schools that admit men."

"Well, if that's true," said Florence, "how can I ever hope to be a doctor?"

Dr. Preston sat forward in her chair. "Times are changing, Florence," she said. "Some brave people are working to help women to go to our medical schools. And when that happens, I think you should be there."

Florence kept looking at Dr. Preston, still hearing her last words. The skin on the back of her neck tingled. Then she stared down at her small hands with their stubby fingers. The zoology teacher said those were good hands to have if you were a scientist. Maybe they would be good if you were a doctor, too.

"Well, Florence," said Dr. Preston. "What do you think?"

"I don't see how it is possible, Dr. Preston," Florence replied quietly. "School costs so much money. My family just doesn't have that much. And, anyway, what medical school would ever let me in?"

"I told you, Florence, times are changing," answered Dr. Preston. "I can't say it will be easy. But hard work, a stout heart, and good friends do a great deal in this world. You will see." She put her arm around Florence.

Florence looked up at Dr. Preston. Here was a good friend. Florence was sure she had a stout heart, and she knew she could work hard. Maybe the dream would come true after all.

Big Decisions

Summer 1893

When classes were finished for the summer, Florence packed her bags and went back to Denver. She could hardly wait to see Papa and Mary. The three of them would be together again.

The little family rented a few rooms in a boarding house and settled down. One hot afternoon a few weeks later, Florence knew it was time to try out her idea.

"Papa, Mary, I want to talk to you both about something, something important," said Florence, as she filled the glasses on the table with lemonade. All the windows of the room were open. Mr. Sabin sat in the easy chair, fanning himself.

"My, you sound serious," Papa said. "Too serious for such a hot day."

"No, Papa," said Florence. "Now that we are all together I have to tell you this news."

"Tell us what?" asked Mary, pinning her long hair up on the top of her head.

"Well—" Florence began. She took a long

sip of lemonade. "I—."

"Yes, go on," urged Papa.

"I want to go to medical school," Florence blurted.

The only sound in the room was the ticking of the clock. Or maybe it was her heart beating, thought Florence. She looked first at Papa and then at Mary.

"Out of the question, my dear," said Papa.

"But, Papa," Florence said, "you were going to be a doctor. Grandmother told me all about it."

"That was different. Young ladies are not doctors," he said firmly. He put down his empty glass. Lifting the straw hat off the hat rack, he placed it on his thick dark hair. "And now, girls, I must be off to see to some business."

As the door closed, Florence turned to her sister. "Mary, what do you think?" she asked.

"I think Papa is right," answered Mary.

"But Mary," said Florence, "Some women do go to medical schools now. Dr. Preston said even more women would be going soon."

"Maybe so," Mary said. "But there is no way you can go."

"But—" began Florence.

"You see, little sister," said Mary, "Papa's mining business just is not doing well. There simply isn't enough money to pay for your medical school training. The idea is impossible. When you finish college, come back here to Denver and teach with me."

Florence stared out of the window. In the distance she could see the white tops of the mountains. A slight breeze stirred the curtains.

"No, you're wrong, Mary," Florence said, turning to face her sister. "It's not impossible. Somehow, some way I am going to medical school. Dr. Preston said it wouldn't be easy, and I guess she's right. But I *will* find a way. You'll see."

No more was said about medical school that summer. By September, Florence had returned to Smith College. She worked harder than ever. Now she was studying chemistry. The professor asked her to join a science club. Members of the club were the best science students at the college. Just for fun they would drink tea from the glass test tubes.

One day Florence was hurrying in the front door of Tenney House. Suddenly someone grabbed her arm. "Slow down, young lady."

Florence looked around to see Dr. Preston smiling at her. "Oh, I'm sorry," said Florence. "I was in such a rush. I didn't even see you. I have a job, you know. Helping at the library."

"I heard about that," answered Dr. Preston. "How would you like another job? You could tutor some girls who are having trouble understanding history and mathematics."

"I would like that a lot," answered Florence. "I could help them after supper each night."

"That won't give you much time to do your own studies, will it?" asked Dr. Preston.

"Oh, I'll manage," said Florence. She began to smile. "Don't you remember? You told me it wouldn't be easy."

For the next two years, Florence continued to work hard. She carefully put all the money she earned in the bank. Now she was about to graduate from college.

"What are your plans for the future, Florence?" asked Dr. Preston as they sat rocking on the front porch of Tenney House. The late night air was warm. Florence took a deep breath. She loved the smell of the lilacs in bloom.

"I'm going back to Denver, Dr. Preston," Florence answered.

"Denver?" asked Dr. Preston. "What about medical school?"

"Oh, I haven't forgotten about medical school," said Florence. "I'm returning to Denver to teach at Wolfe Hall. You remember—that's where Mary and I went to school after Mama died. I am going to save my money and then—with luck—I can go to medical school somewhere."

Dr. Preston stopped rocking. She reached over and took Florence's hand.

"I feel sure you will have luck," she said.

"But you have so much more, too. You are graduating with the highest honors. You are a very intelligent young woman who works hard. By the time you save your money, a medical school will be ready to accept you."

"You sound so sure of that," said Florence.

Dr. Preston nodded. "Haven't I told you about the ladies in Baltimore?"

What ladies in Baltimore, Florence wondered? "No," she answered. "I don't think you have."

"Well, there are three ladies in Baltimore. They are very rich," Dr. Preston explained. "The university in Baltimore—Johns Hopkins University—wants to start a medical school. But the university doesn't have enough money. Can you guess the end of the story?"

"I would guess," answered Florence, "that the three ladies said they would give the university the money if they let women in as students.

"Right you are," said Dr. Preston, laughing.

Florence stood up and began to walk back and forth. She stopped and peered through the dark at her friend. "Well, what do you think?" she asked. "Will they do it? Will the university accept women?"

"No one knows yet," answered Dr. Preston. "But save your money and work hard. By the time you are ready, I wouldn't be surprised if

Johns Hopkins Medical School was ready, too."

Florence sat on the porch railing. Somewhere in the distance, a church bell chimed.

Could she really save enough money for medical school, she wondered? Even if she did, would Johns Hopkins admit any women after all? And most important—would the medical school be ready for Florence Sabin?

New Adventures

Fall 1897

Florence put her suitcases down on the sidewalk. She couldn't believe it. As she gazed up at the dark stone buildings, she just shook her head.

Maybe if I pinch myself, I'll wake up from this dream, she thought. Here she was at Johns Hopkins Medical School. Just a little over three years since she graduated from college. Tomorrow she and fifteen other women in a class of forty would begin their studies. It would be the third freshman class.

All the young women who were students at the medical school lived at a boarding house. They called it "the Hen House." For the first time in years, Florence truly felt at home. Now she could talk about interesting things such as cells and muscles. Everyone worked hard, and the young women all tried to help each other.

One day in April, Florence lay in bed feeling the morning sun on her face. She stretched a moment and turned over. She was still tired from working late the last few weeks.

All of a sudden, she heard the door pushed open. Someone yanked the blankets off. "All right, sleepy head, time to get up!" said a voice. "Time to go hunting."

Florence opened one eye. It was her friend Mabel Glover. "Go away," growled Florence, reaching for the blankets. Then she propped herself up on one elbow. "Hunting? Hunting for what?"

"Frog eggs, Flossie," answered Mabel. No one but Mabel ever called her Flossie. "Don't you remember we said we would hunt frogs' eggs on the first spring day?"

Florence sat up on the edge of the bed. Mabel was taking some clothes out of the closet. Here it was the first day in months when she could sleep a little, and Mabel wanted to hunt for frogs' eggs. Still Florence knew she would go, and she knew she would have a wonderful time.

But it was the next day that something truly wonderful happened. Florence discovered histology. In histology class, students learned about animal tissue by looking at it through a microscope.

Florence walked into the laboratory that morning with the other students. The air was clean. No strong smell of disinfectant like the anatomy laboratory, she noticed. The room was spotless. Florence ran her hand along the edge of the zinc-covered tables that stretched to the back of the room. Microscopes were on the tables. High stools were waiting for the students.

"Good morning, ladies and gentlemen. I am Dr. Mall," announced a small thin man with a mustache. He wore a white laboratory coat and stood very straight. He did not smile.

"Your attention, please," he continued. "You will each take a place by a microscope. With the microscope you will learn to tell a great deal about all different kinds of tissue. If you are careful and pay attention to what you see under the microscope, you will do well."

Florence perched on a tall stool. She slipped one of the prepared glass slides under the lens of the microscope. Then she squinted through the opening.

She could see hundreds of wiggling things, dancing in a little circle. Some of the specks were long. Others were joined in swaying chains.

"Ladies and gentlemen," said Dr. Mall, "you will notice the bacteria that are round and are in pairs. These are called *cocci*. You see that they form chains and clumps. Now notice the long bacteria. They are called *bacilli*."

Florence stared at the cells. She didn't understand what she saw. But as she peered down at those little dancing specks, she was sure that some part of this small world would be her life.

By her second year in medical school, Florence began to know quite a lot about bacteria. Dr. Mall asked her to do work just for him.

"I think you and I should write a paper about your work, Miss Sabin," said Dr. Mall one day. "We should share with other scientists what you have learned. Please begin it right away." Without another word, he left the laboratory.

Florence couldn't believe it. Writing a paper with Dr. Mall. Covering the microscope, she reached for her coat and dashed out the door. Wait till she wrote to Papa. Wouldn't he be proud of her!

Pulling her coat around her, she ran down the street and around the corner and pushed open the door of the Hen House. Mabel was sitting on the bottom step. She held a piece of paper.

"Oh, Flossie, I'm so sorry," she said.

"Sorry," repeated Florence. "Why? I couldn't be happier."

"You mean no one told you?" asked Mabel. "A telegram came this morning. Your father died yesterday."

Florence took the crumpled piece of paper from Mabel. Carefully she smoothed and folded it. Now Papa would never know that she would be a doctor.

She took her handkerchief from her pocket and blew her nose hard. Mabel stood by Florence quietly and put her arm around her. Only Mary was left of their small family, thought Florence. Not much, really. But Mary and friends like Mabel would have to be enough.

The Real Test

Spring 1900

The next two years of medical school passed almost before Florence realized it. Her friend Mabel Glover married her teacher, Dr. Mall. Now Florence visited their home. Sometimes they all went on picnics in the Maryland countryside.

"Dr. Mall is such a stick," said some of the students. But Florence knew he was her friend. Sometimes he stopped to look at her work under the microscope.

"Good work, Miss Sabin," he said.

Florence wrote Mary about the nice things Dr. Mall said about her work. She said it made her feel "fine as silk."

One day Florence was perched on her stool, peering through the microscope. She felt someone stop beside her, and looked up.

Dr. Mall looked at her work as he usually did. He nodded. "Nice," he said. Florence glowed.

"By the way, Miss Sabin," he continued. "I have been looking for someone who would make a model of the base of the brain of a newborn baby."

Florence didn't say a word. Did he really want her to make a model? She was just a student. Only assistants did that kind of work.

"Sir," she began. "Do you truly think I could make such a model?"

Dr. Mall pushed his hands in the pockets of his white laboratory coat. He looked up at the ceiling. "Y—es," he said slowly. "I do believe you could. Would you like to try?"

"Oh, yes sir," Florence replied, softly. "I would indeed!"

Nearly every day after her other work at school was finished, she rushed to the laboratory to work on the model. She knew it would take a very long time to finish. She had to be patient and work very carefully.

Dr. Mall got the brain of a newborn baby who had died at the hospital and brought it to the laboratory. Florence planned what she must do. After many weeks, she was ready to see if her idea would work.

Using a very sharp knife, she traced pieces of the baby's brain onto slices of beeswax. How slowly she had to work. The back of her neck ached, and her fingers stiffened.

Finally she was finished. She was pleased. By putting all the wax pieces together, she saw what looked like a real baby's brain. Now students in medical school could see the model and learn what such a small brain looked like. She hoped Dr. Mall would like it.

The next day, Dr. Mall walked slowly around the table. Sometimes he bent forward to look at the model more carefully.

"Nice, Miss Sabin," he announced. "Yes, very nice indeed."

Florence let out a small sigh. "Thank you, sir," she answered, smiling.

"In fact, the model is so good," said Dr. Mall, "that I believe we must have copies made. The company that makes the best copies is in Germany."

"Germany?" asked Florence. "But that's so far away!"

"So far that you wouldn't take it there yourself?" asked Dr. Mall.

Florence stared blankly at the small man.

Dr. Mall began to smile. "I am saying, Miss Sabin," he explained, "that you shall take your model to Germany yourself. That way you can watch to see that all goes well."

Florence shook her head slowly. "Me? Go to Germany?" she asked. "But how?"

"Oh, that's no problem," answered Dr. Mall. "I know several people who will be happy to pay for your trip. Having such a fine model for students in medical schools is very important. You must leave everything to me."

"Thank you, sir," Florence answered quietly. How wonderful it would be to go to Germany, she thought. But first she must think about graduating and about her internship next year.

An internship is a time of training in which new doctors work with patients in a hospital and with experienced doctors to learn even more about medicine. Florence knew she wanted to work as an intern with Dr. Osler. Her friend, Dorothy Reed, wanted to work with him, too.

Dr. Osler was one of the most famous men in medicine, and working for him was a great honor. Only the very best students were chosen to be his interns. Dorothy and Florence were two of the best students in the class, but they knew that women were seldom given the chance to be interns.

Still, times were changing, they thought. Even the president of the medical school agreed: women should be interns. But only one woman could work with Dr. Osler, he decided.

After hearing the news, Dorothy and Florence walked slowly back to the Hen House. Neither said a word. How could it be, wondered Florence? As she closed the door of her room, she began to cry. She sat on her bed, trying to think what to do.

After awhile, Florence blew her nose and wiped her eyes. She walked down the hall and knocked on Dorothy's door.

"You should be the intern," Florence told her friend. "I will work for Dr. Mall in the laboratory."

"No," answered Dorothy.

"But the president said that only one woman would be allowed to be an intern," Florence reminded her.

"Listen to me, Florence Sabin," said Dorothy, stomping her foot. "You have worked too hard and too long. You are the best student in the class."

"Yes, but—" began Florence.

"No 'but's," answered Dorothy. "The best students work with Dr. Osler. You are going to work with Dr. Osler. I am fourth in the class, so I am also going to work for Dr. Osler. We worked for it and we deserve it. If women are to get any place in this world, they have to defend themselves."

Florence stood looking at her friend. Yes, what Dorothy said made sense, she thought. After all, didn't men and women have the same brains? The important thing was that one's brain be used and used well.

"By golly, you're right, Dorothy," agreed Florence. And she gave her friend a big hug. Then she stepped back and began to grin.

"I think I have an idea," Florence said. "Dorothy, you and I are going calling. Get your coat and follow me." The two girls dashed outside.

As they swung onto the trolley, Dorothy called out, "Florence, where in the world are we going?"

"To see Dr. Mall, of course," she answered. "I just know he'll help us. We'll both work for Dr. Osler yet."

Dr. Mall did help Florence and Dorothy. He convinced the school that both young women deserved to work for Dr. Osler after all.

Then suddenly it was graduation time. That spring day was warm and bright. Florence thought how proud Papa would have been to see her marching in her long black robe with its bright green lining. Only doctors could wear those robes.

But Florence knew there was no time to look back. She must think of the model of the brain now.

Dr. Mall helped her again. On her way to Germany, Florence never let the box with the model packed inside out of her sight. After she arrived, Florence worked hard to learn the strange new language, because she wanted to explain her model. All day she watched and worked with the model makers.

Florence even made some new friends. Somehow she found time to take long walks with them through the beautiful woods. She visited castles and imagined the knights in their armor who might have lived there long ago. The summer months passed all too soon.

Florence hated to leave. The trip sailing back across the ocean would take only a week, and soon she would be at the hospital in Baltimore.

Florence Finds Her Niche

September 1902

What an exciting year 1901 was! But when the time was over Florence knew that the strain of working with sick people was not for her. She was glad she had worked under Dr. Osler, but the quiet and peace of the laboratory must be her life.

Once again, she worked for Dr. Mall. She was an assistant in the Department of Anatomy at the medical school. And now an apartment of her own was what she wanted most.

After some searching, Florence found a small apartment on the second floor of one of the brick row houses. She hung her pictures and made new curtains. It was time to share her happiness with her friends.

"Anyone who performs successful experiments in the laboratory is a good cook," Florence said to her friend, Mabel, one day.

"Oh, is that so?" said Mabel, laughing. "I think you'll just have to prove that to us."

"All right, I will," announced Florence.

"Everyone in the laboratory—and you, too, of course—is invited to dinner on Saturday right after the game.

"What game?" asked Mabel.

"The baseball game, of course," answered Florence. "The Orioles might even win the pennant this year."

"My goodness, Flossie," said Mabel. "I didn't know you were such a fan."

"I try not to miss a single game," added Florence. "But sometimes I am so busy working in the laboratory that I can't help it."

"Well, all right," agreed Mabel. "After the game it is. And we expect the very finest dinner."

"You shall have it," Florence promised. "Don't you worry for a minute."

That Saturday six friends climbed the steep stairs to the apartment. Florence opened the door, and with a low bow she welcomed her guests to her little home.

"You know, I believe you're right, Flossie," said Mabel later. She took a last sip of coffee. "Scientists are good cooks. At least the scientist of this house is a good cook. Don't you agree, Franklin?"

"I do, indeed," answered Dr. Mall. "Steak and lemon pie! Now that's a treat!" He folded his napkin and put it down on the table.

Many more dinner parties followed over the years. Florence loved to cook and loved to be with friends. Most of the time she gave each guest a job to do: one person might set the table, and another might fix the salad. No one minded at all.

Florence was doing important research in the laboratory now. She was trying to find the beginning of the lymphatic system and how it worked. The lympathic system is made up of many tiny vessels that carry fluid called *lymph*. This fluid continuously bathes every cell of the human body. Many people had ideas about how the system worked, but no one really knew.

As always, Florence carefully planned what to do as she tried to find the answer. First, she would go to the library to read what other scientists had done. Most of the books were written in German—how glad she was that she understood German! Then she began to design the tools she would use to do the experiment.

Slowly Florence did each experiment over and over. Her hands were always steady, but her stomach felt as if it were full of butterflies.

As she worked hour after hour, the only noise was the rumble of the traffic on the street outside. Would she really find the answer to the mystery of where the lymphatic system began?

A Friend is Lost

November 1917

The experiments Florence did were a success. She discovered the origin of the lymphatic system. At first some scientists did not believe her when she showed that the lymphatic system started in the tiniest blood vessels. Even so, she won a one-thousand dollar prize for her fine work.

Florence didn't work only in the laboratory. Teaching students how to see bacteria under the microscope was exciting. Often she asked some of her students to her apartment for dinner.

As the years went by, Dr. Mall remained her teacher. What would I ever do without him, Florence wondered? With every big problem, she always knew she could go to him for help.

Then one day, Florence was peering into the microscope. The laboratory was quiet. Someone touched her arm.

Florence looked up to see one of her students. "Dr. Sabin," he said, "someone just called on the telephone. He wants you to go over to Dr. Mall's house right away."

Florence was about to slip another slide under the lens of the microscope, but she stopped. Something was not right, she thought. Why didn't Mabel call herself? What could be wrong?

Florence covered the microscope. After she was outside the laboratory, she hurried down the stairs and out the door. No streetcar was in sight. She decided to run to the house. Her white laboratory coat flapped open.

Puffing as she reached the house, Florence rang the doorbell. A maid opened the big door.

"Oh, Dr. Florence," she said, sniffling. "I'm so glad you've come. It's the doctor. What will the missus do without him?"

Florence put her arm around the large woman. "Dr. Mall?" she asked. "What is the matter?"

"He died, ma'am," the maid answered. "Just an hour ago."

Florence kept patting the big woman. But her own heart throbbed. Died? Impossible. She could not live without him. Then she remembered Mabel.

"Where is Mrs. Mall?" asked Florence.

"In the upstairs sitting room, ma'am," the maid answered.

"I'll just go up," said Florence. "Why don't you fix us all a nice pot of hot tea."

The maid nodded and lumbered down the

narrow hall toward the kitchen.

Florence took a deep breath and climbed the stairs. The afternoon sun lit the sitting room. Two men stood by the window. Mabel sat on a small chair. She turned when Florence came through the door.

"Oh, Flossie," she said quietly, "thank you for coming. I just can't believe it. Franklin wasn't even sick."

Florence put her arm around Mabel. The ticking of the small clock on the mantel was the only sound in the room.

Mabel wiped her eyes with a lace handkerchief. "You know you will have to continue the research in the anatomy laboratory now. You will be named the new head of the department."

But Mabel Mall was wrong. Florence was not asked to be the head of the department. The university gave the job to another professor—a man. Florence's students and many other teachers at the school were angry.

"It doesn't matter," insisted Florence with a shrug.

But as she went about her work in the laboratory, she knew it did matter. How had she failed, she wondered? Other women working in science depended on her. Well, nothing is easy, she reminded herself. Some day the world would realize that women really could be fine scientists.

Honors and Changes

1926

Florence was right. Slowly the world did begin to believe that women could do basic research in science.

Florence earned many honors. She was the first woman to be appointed a professor of anatomy at Johns Hopkins Medical School—her school. She was the first woman elected to life membership of the National Academy of Sciences. In 1925 she was called the greatest living woman scientist and one of the finest scientists of all time.

The next year Florence was asked to start a department at the Rockefeller Institute for Medical Research in New York City. The department would study tuberculosis, a disease that killed thousands of people each year.

Florence was sorry to leave her beloved city of Baltimore. But she was eager to try to find the cure to this terrible disease.

Packing her books, paintings, and Indian rugs Florence moved north to New York City. She rented a comfortable apartment. Each morning she walked a few blocks to the Rockefeller Institute. Her laboratory was on one of the top floors of the large building. Looking out the windows, she could watch the tugboats chug up the East River.

Each day, a few minutes before nine o'clock, Florence stepped off the elevator and opened the door to her laboratory.

"Good morning, everyone," she called cheerfully. "What's new and interesting?"

The young men and women working with her were eager to share their news or a funny story. But within a few minutes, Florence reached for her white laboratory coat. Everyone knew it was time to begin working.

Soon the large laboratory was quiet. Florence bent over a microscope. Her brown curly hair, parted in the middle, was now threaded with grey.

A few hours later, Florence straightened up and checked her watch. "I do believe it's time to have a peanut butter sandwich," she announced.

All the people working in the laboratory sat around a big table. Florence glanced out the window and noticed the sea gulls swooping down to the river for their own lunch—a fat fish, perhaps.

Pulling her sandwich from the paper bag, Florence turned to the young man next to her. "Well, Paul, how did your experiments go this morning?" she asked. "After all these months of work, I think we should be near some important news on the newest part of our work."

"That's how it looks, Dr. Sabin," agreed the young man. "I have just one more test I can do if you think it's really necessary."

Florence took another sip of milk. "You can never be too careful, Paul," she warned. "Yes, you certainly should do that last test."

The light was turning grey in the late afternoon when Paul tapped on Florence's office door.

"Come in, Paul," she said. "I've been waiting for the results of your last test before I start writing a paper about our work."

Paul held a bundle of papers in his hands. "I think you had better look at these charts first, Dr. Sabin," he said.

Florence took the papers and spread them across her desk. She leaned over and looked at them carefully. She shook her head.

"How could it be?" she asked quietly. "We were so sure. Everything else pointed to it."

"I know, Dr. Sabin," agreed the young man. "It's so terrible to think we failed. All those months of work for nothing."

Suddenly Florence straightened up. She turned and put her hands on Paul's shoulders. "Young man," she said, firmly. "I don't ever want you to say or think such a thing again. True, experiments sometimes don't prove what we expected. But that teaches us something, too. We learn important lessons with every experiment we do. Research just takes patience—and lots of it."

"Now, cheer up," she added. "Let's all go home. We'll have a nice dinner and get a good night's sleep. Tomorrow we'll start over."

The next day the little group did start again. As the years quickly passed, Florence and the men and women working with her did important work. They never found a way to control tuberculosis. But they did find out a great deal about the bacterium that causes the disease.

By 1938, the institute officials told Florence

she must retire. I have too much to do, she thought, when she heard the news. But rules were rules.

Florence was sixty-seven years old now. Time to step aside for younger people, she agreed. After all, she had worked hard all her life. She could go back to Denver to live with Mary. From now on she would just take life easy, she decided.

Florence said some sad goodbyes to her friends in New York City. "If you come to visit me," she told them, "you'll find me in my rocking chair."

Even Florence really knew she would never have time to sit in a rocking chair. After she retired, she spoke to scientists at meetings all over the country. Just before the Second World War, she and two men from the United States went to Peking, China, to open a medical center.

One day at the end of the Second World War, in 1945, Mary stood in the doorway of the room Florence used as a study in their Denver apartment. Florence was busily writing at her desk.

"Oh, Florence," said Mary, "will you never rest? What are you up to now?"

"Just putting the finishing touches on this paper," Florence answered, looking up. "It's about some new work some of my former students are doing."

"Well, at least stop a minute for a cup of coffee," pleaded Mary.

"Mary, you're wonderful!" Florence said with a laugh. She plunked down her pen and straightened the pile of papers on the desk. "You're going to make me sit in that rocking chair yet."

This poem hung over the desk of Florence Rena Sabin:

The Bridge Builder

An old man going a lone highway came at the
  evening cold and gray,
To a chasm vast and deep and wide;
The old man crossed in the twilight dim; the sullen
  stream had no fear for him;
But he turned when safe on the other side and built a
  bridge to span the tide.
"Old man," said a fellow pilgrim near, "You are
  wasting your strength building here.
Your journey will end with the ending day. You never
  again will pass this way;
You've crossed the chasm deep and wide; why build
  your bridge at the eventide?"
"Good friend: in the path I have come," he said,
  "there cometh after me today a Youth whose feet
  must pass this way;
This chasm that has been as naught to me, to that
  fair-haired youth may a pitfall be;
He too must cross in the twilight dim; good friend. I
  am building this bridge for him."

Will Allen Dromgoole

Another Adventure

1945

Just a week later, Florence climbed the long flight of stairs leading to the state capitol. She pulled open the heavy wooden doors. Striding down the marble hall, she turned into one of the offices.

"The governor is waiting for you, Dr. Sabin," said the tall man who greeted her. "Please go right in."

Florence walked into the large room. Her hair was almost completely grey now. It was pinned back in a neat bun at the base of her neck.

"Governor Vivian, how kind of you to invite me to see you," said Florence. She shook his hand firmly.

"Not at all," replied the governor. "It is an honor to have you living in your native state of Colorado again."

"Thank you," said Florence. "The last six years here with Mary have been very pleasant."

"Glad to hear it. Yes, indeed," said the governor, coughing a little. "Let me get right to the point," he continued. "The Second World War is over now. People are ready to think about things here in Colorado. I am asking famous people like you to look into certain matters that need some attention. Would you be able to help?"

"What sort of matters do you mean?" Florence quietly asked.

"Well, public health matters," replied the governor. "I am told much of your research was in the area of health."

"Yes, it was," said Florence. "Public health? Yes, I think I can find the time to help. When would you like me to start?"

"Well, ah—" stammered the governor. "Why, I guess you could start as soon as you like, Dr. Sabin. Yes, indeed. That would be just fine."

"Grand," said Florence. "I'll call a meeting tomorrow."

"My, my, Dr. Sabin," said the governor, shaking his head. "You certainly don't waste any time!"

Several weeks later, Florence stood in the governor's office again.

"Public health!" said Dr. Sabin angrily. "We have no public health in Colorado!"

"My good Dr. Sabin," replied the governor. "Whatever do you mean?"

"I mean that babies are sick because the

milk they drink is not pure," said Florence. "I mean that the alleys are filled with trash. Rats and mice are everywhere. I mean—"

"Now wait just a minute," said the governor. "I'm sure it couldn't be all that bad."

"I'm afraid it is much worse," said Florence. "And I don't intend to stand by without doing something about it."

"What are your plans, Dr. Sabin?" asked the governor uneasily.

"I am already working with some men in the legislature to change the health laws," she explained. "And I plan to tell the people of Colorado just how bad health matters are."

"Oh, you mean tell them on the radio," the governor said, smiling.

"I mean tell them myself—in person," said Florence. "I will go to every city and town in Colorado that will have me."

"But my dear Dr. Sabin," said the governor. "You are not a young woman. Surely all that traveling will be hard on you. You must watch your health."

At first Florence said nothing. She buttoned her long brown coat and pulled on her gloves. As she began to open the big door, she turned to the governor. "Sir," she began. "I care about the health of the people of Colorado. If I have anything to say about it, we will have health to match our mountains."

A Wonderful End

1946

Florence worked very hard, but the health laws were not changed that year. Florence was tired.

"I'm discouraged, Mary," she told her sister. "Here I am in the last years of my life, and still nothing comes easily."

Mary began to laugh. "Just have patience," she said. "Remember?"

Florence sat back in her chair and put her feet up on the stool. "How could I ever forget," she said, chuckling. "I guess it just means we'll have to start over again next year."

Florence worked hard with other doctors and public health officials. They made lists of the number of people who died and the reasons for their death. They found out the health problems in all of the sixty-three counties in the state.

One early spring day, Florence reached over to turn off the alarm clock buzzing on the table next to her bed. She sat up and looked out the window. Snow was falling and the wind was blowing.

Suddenly the telephone rang. Mary answered it. "Florence," she called. "It's the state patrol. They say the roads are just too slippery to drive north today."

Florence reached into her closet for her heavy wool dress. "Now, Mary," she said. "Just tell the officer that the people living there are expecting me. I'm sure we'll get there if we start right away."

A few minutes later, Mary stuck her head into the bedroom. "The officer said he would pick you up in half an hour," she said. "But I think he is sure you're just a little crazy."

Florence began to laugh as she combed her hair. "The officer is probably right, Mary," she said. "But this matter of public health—real public health—is important."

The drive that day was slow. Several times patrolmen stopped the car to warn them of the bad roads ahead. But Florence just shook her head. "No, we must go on," she said.

By noon, Florence and the officer climbed the slippery steps of the town's high school. They shook the snow from their coats and went into the cafeteria. The room was full of people.

After taking off her coat and drinking a cup of hot coffee, Florence walked to the front of the room. She began to speak. She told how important it was to have pure milk. She told how everything used to prepare milk must be clean.

Most of the men and women listened and clapped. But a small group of men in the back of the room grumbled to each other.

"Gentlemen," said Florence to the men. "What seems to be troubling you?"

"I'll tell you what's troubling us," one man said. He stood up and leaned against the chair in front of him. "We're sick and tired of your telling us what to do."

"You bet," agreed the other men sitting nearby.

"We're dairymen," the man explained. "And we know our business. Why, who are you to tell us to wash our overalls? Who are you to tell us to close off our haylofts just because a little hay and dust falls down onto the milking area?"

Suddenly a woman jumped up and faced the group of men. "I'll tell you who she is, Dan Jones. She's Dr. Sabin, and she cares about us and about our babies."

"I don't need to listen to you, Emily Brown," the man insisted.

"Well, you'd better listen," continued the woman. "I'm tired of the milk in this town being so dirty you can't drink it. Dr. Sabin is right. It's high time we had health to match our mountains."

Dr. Sabin raised her hand. "Now, everyone," she said. "Please. I didn't come here to start a fight. I came here to start a war—a war against dirt and bacteria. We must help each other if we are to win this war."

The men and women in the room nodded. "We're with you all the way," one man called out.

The next year the new public health laws were passed. Florence was seventy-six years old, and she had a new job: The mayor of Denver asked her to be the manager of health for the city.

Florence worked to make the city a healthier place in which to live.

"Denver General Hospital is a public disgrace," Florence stated. "Just look at it! Window

shades torn, no screens around the patients' beds, no clean sheets, and the toilets don't work."

The mayor looked at Florence and smiled. "Well, if I know you, Dr. Sabin," he said, "these problems won't last long."

Florence never stopped working. "Work keeps you young," she said.

But now Mary was sick and needed her care. Florence spent most of her time with Mary. Many nights Florence slept in a chair next to her bed.

Tired from nursing Mary, Florence got sick. She was taken to the hospital with pneumonia. But soon she seemed to get well and wanted to go home.

The day was warm for October in 1953. Florence sat watching the World Series on television; the Yankees were ahead. That's just as it should be, she thought. After all, they're the best team. Then she realized how thirsty she was; a nice cool glass of water would taste good. She pulled herself out of her chair and walked toward the kitchen. Suddenly she fell to the floor. Florence Sabin died of a heart attack.

In 1864 the U.S. Congress passed a law allowing each state to place statues of two famous citizens of the state in Statuary Hall in the Capitol, in Washington, D.C. Colorado presented a large bronze statue of Florence Rena

Sabin, cast by Joy Buba, to the 85th Congress in 1958.

The statue shows Florence sitting on a stool. Her arm rests on a book called *Colorado Health Laws*. A microscope stands on a small table nearby. The words below the statue read: teacher, scientist, humanitarian.

Bibliography

Books

Bevine, Frances F. *The Amiable Baltimoreans.* New York, E. P. Dutton & Co., 1951.

Bluemal, Elinor. *Florence Sabin: Colorado Woman of the Century.* Boulder, Colorado, University of Colorado Press, 1959.

O'Neill, William L. *The Women's Movement; Feminism in the United States and England.* London, George Allen and Unwin, Ltd., 1969.

Phelan, Mary Kay. *Probing the Unknown: The Story of Dr. Florence Sabin.* New York, Thomas Y. Crowell Co., 1969.

Yost, Edna. *American Women of Science.* New York, J. B. Lippincott Co., 1943.

Private Collections

"Folio, Florence R. Sabin, 1903–1959." James Waring Library, University of Colorado, Medical Library, Denver, Colorado.

"Sabin Publications, 1937–1953." James Waring Library, University of Colorado, Medical Library, Denver, Colorado.

Articles by and about Florence Sabin

"Enterprise Unlimited," radio program, sponsored by U.S. National Bank of Denver, Vol. 1, No. 14, 1948-49.

Sabin, Florence. "The People Win for Public Health in Colorado." 1947.

Walker, Harold. "Academy of Sciences Opens to a Woman." *N.Y. Times Magazine*, 17 May 1925.

Wiggam, Albert E. "A Woman Crusader of Science." *N.Y. Herald Tribune*, 1 December 1929.

"Health Bill Killed in 1945—Sacrificed Public Health for Politics." *Denver Post*, 1 April 1945.